THIS NOTEBOOK BELONGS TO

Made in the USA
Monee, IL
28 December 2022

23795058R00069